Untitled

Timiro Elizabeth

BookLeaf Publishing

Presentation by *BookLeaf Publishing*

Web: www.bookleafpub.com

E-mail: info@bookleafpub.com

ISBN: 9789358369007

First edition 2023

DEDICATION

This collection is dedicated to: Mommie, Grandma, Daddy, and God.

Known

Have you ever tried to be known?
Like the ancestors we know nothing about.
Or the leaders who made something of
themselves
To show what our people have achieved.
But in this generation we take the past for
granted
So Once again other races see us as a peon
This is not something to be proud of.
But does it make a difference anymore?
No one seems to care but the few achievers we
barely notice
Like Malcolm X once said "X, stands for the
unknown".
So will blacks stay unknown?
Or will we overcome the negativity.
And try to show what the hard work some has
put out for us to live up to.
So now it's all up to you to show the world we
can be…KNOWN!

I Wish It Was That Simple

I Wish It Was That Simple
I wish it was that simple.
To deny our love, you know it's true.
But you are better at this game then me.
I've tried to get past each level with only 4 lives
Yet I'm constantly dying. Losing one at a time.
Tve been stuck here too. Not even an extra life
now
To help me get out of this game.
I
I wish it was that simple...
To deny the other women who have gotten what
I wanted.
But it is way harder than you try and make it out
You've won this game plenty of times.
Then why are you stuck on which way to go
now?
You played this pant about 20 times.
Can't you remember?
I wish it was that simple...
To deny your lies.
But I was blinded by love. That's why I cry.
I believe your every word as if they were my
own.

They aren't though, so why do I act as if they
are?
Why do I seem to torture myself over you?
In the end I will get hurt. Then why do I bother?
Why don't you just say it?
It's not that hard. Why do you act as if I'll hurt
you again?
Rejection? Pain? Betrayal? Well guess what you
have put me through it all.
And I still love you. That's how strong these
feelings are.
Face it.
Only now: I wish it was that simple...

Can You?

Can you tell me you love me and mean it?
Or will you reject me and say not at the
moment?
Can you make my body weak with your need?
Or make me sick of your laid back scene?
Can you put any other girl above me and still
remind me everyday that you and only you will
always love me?
Or will I have to find out you are trying to lose
my trust?
Can you caress my very soul?
Or will you stroke it to rough?
Can you give me the benefit of the doubt?
Or make me scream and shout?
Can you fulfill my every need without a second
thought?
Or try and pass me by like I'm a waste of any
heart?
Can you tell me the truth by looking me in the
eye?
Or reverse it and lie?
Am I asking for too much?
I'm sorry but that's just how I roll. Like Luther
said "Everyone needs a love no doubt." So I will
sing that until I find the one. I may sound

desperate and pitiful but this is what I want. To
me it is either accept it or reject it. I wont.
Can you?   5

Toxic

Just because someone doesn't love you the way
you want doesn't mean they don't love you with
all they have." - Anonymous

20 bitches. 50 hoes. The conversation started at
12:30 AM and it ended at 1:00. In the span of 30
minutes. I had been called 20 bitches and 50
hoes. How could he talk to me in such a
way? After I cried all those tears and begged
him to understand, he did not listen. In the span
of 30 minutes my world came crashing down.
Maybe I should have lied? Stupid me! What I
should have done was have sex with unprotected
the day after I had sex with the other man. Then,
I could have said this baby was his. You know,
that would have protected my heart from being
broken. And his. Shit, this was his entire fault
anyway.
He doesn't get it. All I ever wanted was for him
to know my heart and give me the emotional
security I needed. He couldn't do that. How did
things get to this point? I really can't say. It's all
been a blur to me. What I do know is what I'm
feeling. I love him. Does he not see

that? Who cares if I got pregnant by another
man? Abortion is out of the question! I
understand that six years was a long time for us
to be together and now it has come to a halt. The
love of my life caused all of this. All he had to
do was love me the way I needed.ifhe would
have shown me more when I asked for it.
I would have NEVER given in to temptation and
found comfort in another man's arms.
The father of my child won't be around, but the
love of my life should. I need him. I can tell he
has a slight case of amnesia. Is it possible for
him to have amnesia of the heart?
Seriously, he acts as though he never meant
anything to me! You know what forget him! I
don't need him or his love. I will have my child
and he or she will be all I'll ever need.

————

I picked up the phone at 12:30 expecting to hear
her beautiful voice and I was ready to say I love
you to her before I went to bed. Two minutes in
and a bomb went off.
She said, *I'm pregnant. The baby is not yours.
I'm so sorry."
I dropped the phone from my ears as an aching
pain consumed my heart. I had never felt this
before. Was this real? The pain in my chest
reminded me that it was. I grabbed the phone

from off the floor and before I could think twice
or hear an explanation, I snapped.
How the FUCK could she do this to me? After
all I had given her. I'm paying her BILLS and
providing her with any and everything her heart
desired. I make damn near six figures a year, and
I graduated college less than a year ago. A
successful black man. That's what I am. Didn't
they say behind every great man stands a strong
woman? I thought I had that in her.
Blah. Blah Blah.
I've heard this all before. I was more than
emotionally invested in our relationship. For six
years I gave her my all. I gave her everything I
had. And it led her to cheat on me and get
pregnant by another man? I did that? If she
loved me so much why couldn't she just get rid
of it and maybe we could get past this.
You know what we CAN'T get past this. I could
take care of the child as my own, but every time
I may look in that child's face, all I would be
able to see is her betrayal. Her lies. Our love. I
would look at her kid and see everything we
used to have.
Shut up! Shutthefuckup!
I was drained. My emotions were running high.
She didn't get it. How could she not see what
she has thrown away? I couldn't take hearing her
voice anymore.

Goodbye.

At 1:00 AM, I ended the conversation and that chapter of my life.

"Strangers"

The Berenstain Bears and my mother taught me
to never talk to strangers, but I hated ignoring
people in need. I saw the same man every day
for weeks, and he was always sitting at the same
spot on the corner. Everyone always walked past
him as if he did not exist. I had no idea why. I
was determined that tomorrow I was going to
finally give him some food or at the least a hello.
The next day my mother was preparing my
lunch for school, I told her to make extra
because I was hitting puberty and needed to
nourish my growing body. She laughed but
gladly agreed. I was ecstatic. I could not wait to
see the smile on the man's face. I left out of the
house and made my way towards school. As I
hit the corner, there was the man. His sign said
he needed food. I handed him my extra lunch
bag. He smiled brightly and nodded his head. I
was sure he would say thank you, but I could
accept his smile as gratitude.
I missed school for two days because I came
down with a small cold, but the entire time I
wondered what the man was going to eat or
whether he was there or not. My mother made
me an extra lunch to take to back to school with

me; I was glad that she did not think to ask why again. I ran out of the house and towards the corner where the man was. As I got closer I saw him sitting there once more. I smiled and handed him the lunch. He took the lunch and smiled sadly.

"What's wrong?" I asked concerned. Instead of him responding he just shook his head and patted my hand. I heard the school bell ring, so I waved good bye and ran to my school. I hope he was okay.

A month passed with me giving the man lunch and a smile. Today I came to school and I brought a card and a better lunch to brighten his day. As I neared the corner, I did not see him. Instead I saw his hat turned upside down with a folded paper inside.

It read:

Dear Young Man,

Actions speak louder than words ever could and you showed me with you actions how much you cared for a stranger like me. I have been deaf for the last year and lost my job because of it. I stopped smiling because I am also dying of cancer. I can tell my time is near. I did not want you to see me this way, so I left. I don't have much to leave you but this hat and my undying appreciation. You made a sick deaf man very happy. Stay good young man.

I left the card and the lunch, tucked his note in my pocket, and placed his hat on. I smiled sadly, and slowly walked towards school.

Trapped

Etta James and Billie Holliday for a rainy day outside was just what I needed. The passion and roughness in their voices gave me life. I felt like they've dealt with all of the world's pain but somehow through it all was able to make something beautiful. Like the rose that grew from concrete. I was so glad school was canceled because of the storm watch; it gave me more time to ease my mind. School, basketball, track, the list goes on. I hardly have time to chill out. As I closed my eyes to listen to drift into another world there were two light taps on my bedroom door. It never fails. I can never have peace.

"Come in!" I yelled.

"Jeremy you know this is not the time to be locked up in your room." My Dad said. I opened my eyes slowly and eyed his 6'0 frame towering over the side of my bed. His almond eyes were red and his skin was a lot paler than normal. His jet black hair was unkempt but with a simple run through with his finger, his mane would be fine.

"The hurricane is getting closer and closer. You need to come downstairs in the basement with me and your mother. This is a time where we all

need to be together. Do you understand?" My
dad knows I hated to be around him for a long
period of time. To be stuck in the basement with
my mother and him would be pure torture. I
understood their concern. I was browsing the
internet earlier and read that Hurricane Sandy
was planning to do a number on New York and
New Jersey. Any day now New York City was
going to look like New Orleans did in 2005,
maybe worse. I was in denial believing this
would pass and everything would go back to
normal in a week or so. Suddenly the light
started flickering and I heard something crash
outside. It was obvious that God was showing to
dismiss that last thought, because this hurricane
was very much real.

"Jeremy come on! Come now!" I hopped out of
the bed and ran out of my room following
behind my Dad. We dashed down two flights of
stairs making it to the basement apartment in our
townhouse. As soon as I closed the basement
door the room went black.

"You know! I'm so tired of you being so
stubborn! Just imagine what would have
happened if I did not go upstairs to get you!
Imagine!" All I knew was that he needed to chill
out. There was no need to dwell on what would
have happened. The fact remains is that he did
get me and I was safe.

"Khan…calm down. I know you are upset but we have to stay calm. He is here now. Alright?" My mother said as she lit candles around the apartment. How were we going to survive with no power? I grabbed my cell phone and just my luck it was dying.

"How are we supposed to know what is going on if we have no power?" I asked my mother. She looked at me and shook her head.

"I have my handheld radio, it takes batteries and I also have flashlights and tons of candles. I also have a portable charge that we can hook into our cell phones, but I doubt that we have service." I loved my mother, she always stayed calm even when she had a right to panic or freak out. She was the definition of a strong black woman. Once the room was completely lit I saw that they spent all day preparing for this hurricane while I was locked in my room. She had two air mattresses one for them and one for me, quilts, blankets, canned foods, water, board games, and two huge first aid kits.

"When did you guys grab all these things?"

"I went to the store the other day and gathered three months of supplies so can be okay with whatever happens."

"I feel like I'm a part of The Walking Dead. Would I be considered Carl in this situation?" My mother chuckled but my dad looked at me

and started cursing under his breath in
Vietnamese. Although I was cracking jokes, I
knew I could not last three months in this
situation. My dad and I could not get along. I
hated when he cursed me in Vietnamese.
Especially when I was trying to lighten the
mood.
"Chante, don't encourage his behavior. He
should be grateful that your or I went to these
lengths to make sure he was comfortable and not
having to worry." Why did he always have to
ruin the mood?
"Why are you always against me?" I yelled at
him.
"Against you? Why are you always against me?
I try my hardest to be a good father to you but
all you do is push me away! I'm sick of your shit
Jeremy! You need to learn to respect me!" I
couldn't respect him, he was always angry and I
hated how my mother always catered to him like
he was the child. My mother always stood idle
and watched us argue. I wish she would stick up
for me more, if not me, then herself.
"We are urging people to stay where they are!
The storm is getting closer at a rapid pace. I
hope everyone is staying tuned while we give
lives updates. So far, most areas that are not
along the coastline have not been hit terribly, but
that does not mean we are out of the clear. There

will be major flooding in most parts of the city, and MTA has shut down until further notice. All flights have been cancelled…" A man said through my mother's handheld radio. Reality finally sunk in. I was trapped in my basement with my mother and father. The worst part was that I had no idea for how long and whether or not we were going to survive this. As fear slowly crept inside me, I looked over at my father and anger soon replaced that feeling. I needed God to get me out of this one. I closed my eyes, got on my knees and started praying silently.

"What are you doing? Get up?" My dad yelled. I looked at him and then my mother.

The anger took over, and I said, "I'm praying that God gets me out of here, because of honestly I would rather fend for myself out there, than be stuck down here with you." My dad face instantly changed from angry to defeated and hurt. My mother's mouth fell open and I felt no remorse to what I had said. It was cold, but he was no more tired than I was of the bullshit. I got off my knees and went to sit in a corner. I had no idea how I was going to get through this.

Illusion of Love

What do you do when the illusion of love fades?
Their whispers, that used to tickle your eardrum
have now become violent screams of
Bitch.
Hoe.
Pussy.
You combat it with songs of love in your head,
slowly causing those screams to dwindle.
What do you do when the illusion of love fades?
The person you used to see through rose colored
glasses begins to falter.
Now every time you look through the lens, all
you see are hues of red.
Through this lens, you begin to see someone
who once seemed so familiar start to look
foreign. And then you believe your eyes must be
playing tricks on you.
You toss the glasses to the side, rub your eyes,
blink a few times, and try to regain focus.
You begin the process of mourning at the
realization nothing has changed...
And could no longer tell if the tightness in your
chest was from anxiety, love, or fear.

You can't accept what your eyes are seeing,
what your heart is feeling, nor what your body is
taking.
Numbness becomes you...

Soul-Tied

Since I'm being open...
Why do I keep smelling the scent of you?
It consumes me and I soon get lost in the
thought of us
How dare you
Become embedded in me so deeply
Then leave, while every part of me is still
connected to you
And I can't explain why...

Soul-Mated

One month in we were past infatuation.
We were on a high just from getting to know one
another.
We figured making it official was the best thing
to match the feeling in our hearts.
Neither of us concerned on the strength of our
friendship and foundation,
we did not tread lightly
and
things got real heavy
really fast
soon
fear settled in
And
we started running from the intensity of
us
being able to not
succumb
wanting
craving
control
power
but in love...

Unrequited Love

I don't know what it'll take but I'm still not
satisfied. I feel crazy
I can't take the fact of you having any other
person feeling this same way.
Not a year later.
The way you would take my breath away.
The way time would stop when I looked in your
eyes.
The way my chest felt pressed against yours.
Heart to heart. Beating erratically.
Often, I feel you. As if you never left.
I can't shake you.
No matter what I discover about you.
I still get those same feelings in my chest.
Breath still catches and my heart stops at the
memory of the way you called me 'Honey'. PB
& J's and Oatmeal. Your schtick. The way your
jaw clenches when you're quietly angry. The
way you patted and rocked me when we
cuddled.
I'm foolish for admitting that you've gotten me
this way.
But does it matter when I couldn't even have sex
without envisioning you?
To the point I just stopped completely.

It's not fair.
I want to be over you. So bad and time isn't
helping. The truth isn't helping.
I haven't been this out of wack since I was a
teenager.
I don't know what you did to me.
It's maddening cause I've never worked so hard
to kill my emotions and they only remain the
same even after all the pain, lies, and betrayal.

Love Him

I love him
He loves me
We have that love that'll last for eternity
I was always yours to have
You were always mine to keep
Don't underestimate our love
For it remains a mystery
I love Him
And He loves me
There is no end to our love story.

Love You

First, it was SORRY because I wasn't enough for
you
Then it changed to I AIN'T SORRY NO MORE
because I was like "Fuck You"
Then one day I was sitting at home and I wrote a
simple LOVE POEM
You know since I was thinking of you..
That night IN MY DREAMS I asked you to,
"Hold me tighter, kiss me longer."
Didn't realize it was all a dream until you were
no longer there.
Then my dreams became a reality.
Something told me you would always be there.
Didn't you know OUR LOVE would last for
eternity?
One day out of the blue
You turned on me and love did too!
"Forget you!" The two of you said in unison.
Why?
Why?
Why?
I asked in total despair.
Love turned and said to me,
*It takes a fool to learn, that love don't love
nobody."

You & Love walked away, hand in hand...
Instead of me saying, "Come back! Stay."
Inside I knew it was okay.
I know we'll cross paths again someday...

The Truth (Prolouge)

As I read the contents of the letter, I was aware of the smile on my face. I was ecstatic, I mean after all these years of searching and rejection; from almost a hundred different people with the last name Hunter, my mother had finally reached out to me!

At 26, I've lived a life that requires an age way beyond my years. Despite, being in the face of adversity evervday of my life, I always prevailed. Like me having my son at 11, by a 16 year old boy named London, who I thought I was in love with.

You see being a foster child and being moved from home to home all my life, gave me the need to always search and desire someone that could possibly be permanent. Yet, because I was searching in all the wrong places, no one ever stayed for long. I used to get depressed at the thought that my parents abandoned me, literally, ever since I cried into this world. It hurt, but those thoughts and my depression, I couldn't allow them to keep my life at a stand still. Someone once told me that the only constant in life was change. I knew then that, I had to keep it moving...the moving stopped when I was 17.

I became a success all by myself and from the
motivation to do better for my son. My son,
Sean, and I ended up living in shelters until I
was able to get a job and get us a little studio
apartment which we stayed in for 5 years while I
attended Roosevelt University and attained a
B.A. in English.
Now, I am currently working on achieving my
Masters in Communications and African
American Studies. All alone I did these things
when I was constantly set up to fail. Of course,
through the good, the bad, and the ugly, my
bitterness towards the life I was given had faded
away. Most people may wallow in self-pity and
hate. I obviously felt and did the opposite. I
firmly believe and stand by what doesn't kill you
makes you stronger.
My mother, Sandra Hunter, simply says in the
letter:
Dear Tiffany,
My Name is Sandra Hunter. I am your biological
mother. I know you may be confused as to why
am FINALLY reaching out to you. Basically, I
love you and despite what you may think. And I
can explain and tell you everything you need to
know. Please write back, if you get this.
four mother,
Sandra Hunter

Yes, I felt like more could have been said, but I still held more meaning and purpose then anyone would ever know.

"Ma, why are you smiling? What is that?" Sean asks, as he walks up behind me to get a glance at the letter. Tears of joy started to roll down my face.

"It's a letter, from my mother." Sean didn't respond. I looked up at him and he had a look of absolute shock.

"Your mother?" His features then turned to a scowl. His body language got tense.

"Yes" I said nodding my head. Sean turned and walked out the room. He was upset. Especially, because he was a part of my struggle all his life, and he hated the grandparents he never knew for putting me through it. I was angry deep down, but happiness eliminated that emotion for now. Sean was too young to see it my way. I saw this letter as one step close to the closure. One step closer to the truth.

Deaf

Deaf?
Gotta be.
I scream so loud.
Yet nobody hears me.
No one reacts.
Hello?
Anybody home?
Deaf?
Gotta be.
I scream louder.
Feeling as though I'm at my wits end.
LISTEN
SOMEONE PLEASE
I'm lonely
I'm insecure
No one loves me
My mother is a crack addict
My father left me too early
I can still feel his skin...so cold.
Just like my soul.
It weakens all my bones!
DO YOU HEAR ME?
I loved a boy.
Found out he was crazy, he popped pills daily.

Then there was that guy who kept me on the
side.
I wanted more, needed more...so I said...
I LOVE YOU, BUT..
PLEASE SOMEONE HELP ME
DO YOU NOT UNDERSTAND?
I'm a product of what He made me.
I would look to Him.
I don't think He is real.
He hasn't helped me yet.
All He has caused me is pain and regret.
HELLO?
DO YOU HEAR ME?
Silence.
Deaf?
Gotta be.
It falls on deaf ears.
The silence so loud.
Hello?
Anybody home?
No one is there...
No one is ever there...
Silence.
It consumes me.
I look in the mirror.
I see you, Dad.
Not me.
You.
Then, I see myself.

I don't need their help.
Yes, I got this.
We got this.
Deaf?
No.
I can hear me...

,

But

Wait

There's

More...